A Book of

BABY
NAMES

Classic and Contemporary
Names for Your Baby

JANE P. RESNICK

A good name is better than riches.
MIGUEL DE CERVANTES

SMITHMARK

© 1994 SMITHMARK Publishers, Inc.

This edition is published in 1994
by SMITHMARK Publishers, Inc.,
16 East 32nd Street, New York, NY 10016.

SMITHMARK books are available for bulk purchase for
sales promotion and premium use. For details write or call
the manager of special sales, SMITHMARK Publishers, Inc., 16 East 32nd
Street, New York, NY 10016; (212) 532-6600.

Produced by Ripinsky + Company
Cover and text design by Marysarah Quinn
Cover photo © 1993 Solomon M. Skolnick
Edited by Sara Colacurto

Library of Congress Cataloging-in-Publication Data
Resnick, Jane Parker
A book of baby names : classic and contemporary
names for your baby / Jane P. Resnick
p.   cm.
ISBN 0-8317-0668-6 : $6.98
1. Names, Personal—Dictionaries.   I. Title
CS2377.R47 1994
929.4'4'03—dc20
93-2066 CIP

Printed in the United States of America

10 9 8 7 6 5 4 3 2 1

Girls' Names

Abigail (*Hebrew*): A father's joy. Abby, Abbie.

Adelaide (*German*): Noble and of good cheer. Ada, Adeline, Heidi.

Adele (*French*): Form of Adelaide.

Adrienne (*French*): Feminine form of Adrian. Latin place name. Adrien, Adrianne, Adeiana.

Agatha (*Greek*): Good. Agathe, Agathy, Aggie.

Agnes (*Greek*): Pure, gentle. Ines, Inez, Agnesa, Nessa.

Aileen (*Irish*): Light. Form of Helen. Ayleen, Aila, Ailene, Alene.

Aisha (*Arabic*): Woman. Aiesha, Ayeisha, Ieaisha, Ieesha, Yiesha.

Alanna (*Irish*): Rock, or comely. Feminine form of Alan. Alana, Lana.

Alexandra (*Greek*): Defender of men. Feminine form of Alexander. Alexine, Alexia, Alix, Xandra.

Alexis (*Greek*): Helper. Alessa, Lexi, Alexa, Alexia.

Alice (*Old German*): Noble. Alicia, Alissa, Ali, Alyce.

Alida (*Latin*): Small, winged one. Aleda, Aleta, Elida, Dela.

Alisa (*Hebrew*): Great happiness. Alisah, Alissa, Alyssah.

Aliya (*Arabic*): Highborn.

Allegra (*Italian*): Lively; joyful. Alegra, Legra.

Allison (*French*): Diminutive of Alice. Alison, Alyson, Allisann, Allie.

Alma (*Latin*): Nurturing; kind. (*Italian*): Soul. Almah, Allma.

Althea (*Greek*): With power to heal. Altha, Althia, Elthea, Thea.

Amber (*French*): Jewel name. Ambar, Amberly, Ambur.

Amanda (*Latin*): Much loved. Mandy, Amandi, Amata, Mandaline.

Amelia (*Old German*): Industrious. Amalea, Amalie, Ameliya, Amilia.

Amina (*Arabic*): Honest. Aminah.

Amira (*Arabic*): Highborn girl. Ameera, Amirah, Meera, Merah.

Amy (*Latin*): Beloved. Aimee, Aimie, Ami, Amia, Amiah, Esma, Esme.

Anastasia (*Greek*): Resurrection. Ana, Asia, Stacey, Tasia.

Anika (*African*): Sweetness of face. Anacka, Anikee, Annaka.

Anita (*Spanish*): See Ann.

Andrea (*Latin*): Womanly. Feminine form of Andrew. Andee, Andrianna, Andria, Andy.

Angela (*Greek*): Heavenly messenger. Angelica, Angelina, Angelique, Angie.

Ann English form of Hannah (*Hebrew*): Grace. Anne, Anna, Annie, Anya, Nan.

Annabel (*Latin*): Graceful and beautiful. Annabelle, Anabella, Anabel.

Annemaria Combination of Ann and Mary. Annamarie, Annmaria, Annmarie.

Annette Diminutive form of Ann. Anet, Anett, Aneta.

Antonia (*Latin*): Priceless. Feminine form of Anthony. Antoinette, Nettie, Tony.

April (*Latin*): Opening up. Averel, Averill, Avril, Avrill.

Arabella (*Latin*): Answered prayer. Ara, Arabel, Arabela, Arabelle.

Arden (*Latin*): Enthusiastic. Ardeen, Ardena, Ardin.

Aretha (*Greek*): Virtue. Areta, Arette, Aretta.

Ariana (*Welsh*): Like silver. Ariane.

Ariel (*Hebrew*): Lioness of God. Arielle.

Arlene (*Celtic*): Pledge. Arleen, Arline, Arlena, Arleta, Lena, Lina.

Ashanti (*African*): Tribal name. Ashanta, Ashantee, Ashaunte, Ashaunti.

Ashley (*Old English*): Ash tree. Ashlie, Ashleigh, Ashly, Ashlee.

Asia Name of the continent. Originally sunrise, east.

Astra (*Latin*): Of the stars. Asta, Astera, Asteria, Astrea.

Athalia (*Hebrew*): The Lord is exalted. Atalia, Athalee, Athalie.

Atifa (*Arabic*): Affection. Ateefa.

Audrey (*Old English*): Noble strength. Audra, Audree, Audrea, Audry.

Aurora (*Latin*): Dawn. Aurore, Ora, Rora, Zora.

Autumn Season name.

Bailey (*Old English*): Law enforcer. Bailee, Baily.

Barbara (*Latin*): Stranger. Babs, Barbi, Barbra, Barbro, Bobbie, Basha.

Beatrice (*Latin*): Bringer of gladness. Beatrix, Bea, Beatrisa, Trixie.

Belinda (*Spanish*): Beautiful. Bella, Linda, Bellinda, Lindy.

Bernadette (*French*): Feminine form of Bernard. Bear; courageous. Berna, Bernadene, Bernettee, Bernita, Bernie.

Bernice (*Greek*): Bringer of victory. Barrie, Berenice, Bunny.

Bertha (*Old German*): Bright. Berthe, Berti, Berta.

Beth (*Hebrew*): House. Short form of Elizabeth. Betty, Betsy.

Bethany Biblical place name. Bethanie, Bethanne, Bethanny.

Betty Diminutive of Elizabeth (*Hebrew*): Pledged to God. Bett, Bette, Bettina, Bettine.

Beverly (*Old English*): Beaver stream. Place name in Yorkshire. Bev, Beverle, Verlie, Buffy.

Bianca (*Italian*): White. Blanca, Blancha.

Blaine (*Irish*): Slender. Blane, Blayne.

Blair (*Scottish*): Place name for a plain. Blaire.

Bliss (*Old English*): Intense happiness. Blisse, Blyss.

Blythe (*Old English*): Joyous; carefree. Blithe.

Bonnie (*Scottish*): Good; fair of face. Bonne, Bonnebell, Bonny, Bunny.

Brandy A type of liquor. Brandi.

Brenda (*Old English*): Burning. Possibly Norse for sword. Brenn, Brennda, Brenndah.

Brenna (*Irish*): Black-haired. Bren, Brenne, Brennah.

Briana Feminine form of Brian (*Irish*): Strong. Brana, Breena, Briny, Bryn, Bryanna.

Bridget (*Irish*, Brigit; *French*, Brigitte; *Scandinavian*, Brigitta): Strength. Bergete, Briget, Brigit, Brita, Britt.

Brittany (*Latin*): From England. Brittny, Britt, Brittini, Brett, Brittnee.

Brooke (*Old English*): Place name. From a stream. Brook, Brooks.

Caitlin (*Irish* for Catherine): Kaitlin, Caitlan, Kaitlan.

Cala (*Arabic*): Castle.

Camille (*Latin*): Attendant. Cam, Cammie, Cammilla, Milli, Milee.

Candace (*Greek*): Glowing white. Candice, Candee, Candi, Dacey, Kandace, Kandiss.

Candida (*Latin*): White. Candi, Candide, Candy.

Cara (*Latin*): Dear. Kara, Carina, Karine, Karrie.

Carey (*Welsh*): Castle dweller. Kerry, Kerrie.

Carmen (*Latin*): Song. Carmella, Carmelle, Carmilla, Carmelita.

Carol (*Old German*): Strong. Carole, Karol, Carola, Carrol, Carroll, Caryl.

Caroline Feminine form of Charles (*Old German*): Little; womanly. Carolyn, Carleen, Caralyne, Karolyne.

Cassandra (*Greek*): Prophetess. Cassie, Cass, Kassandra, Kassie, Sondra, Zandra.

Catherine (*Greek*): Pure. Catarina, Cathleen, Cathryn, Cathy.

Cecilia (*Latin*): Blind. Cecily, Celia, Ceil, Cecile, Sisely.

Chandra (*Sanskrit*): Like the moon. Candra, Shandra.

Chanel Name of famous French designer and perfume. Channel, Shanel, Shanelle, Shannel.

Chantal (*French*): Stony place. Chantelle, Shantal, Shantelle.

Charity (*Latin*): Love; affection. Charissa, Cher, Cherry.

Charlotte Feminine form of Charles (*French*): Lottie, Charlotta, Carlotta.

A good name keeps its lustre in the dark.

ENGLISH PROVERB

Charmaine (*Latin*): Clan name. Sharmaine, Sharman, Sharmane.

Chelsea (*Old English*): Landing place on a river. Chelsey, Chelsie.

Cheryl Familiar form of Charlotte. Charyl, Sharil, Sherill, Sheryl.

Christina Feminine form of Christian (*Greek*): Anointed. Christine, Kristina, Krystyna.

Claire (*Latin*): Bright. Clare, Clair, Clara, Claretta, Clarice, Clarissa.

Claudia (*Latin*): Clan name. Feminine form of Claude. Claudette, Claudine, Claudeen.

Colette (*French*): Diminutive for Nicolette. Collette, Coletta.

Colleen (*Irish*): Girl. Coleen, Colene, Coline.

Constance (*Latin*): Constancy; firmness. Connie, Constantina, Constantine.

Cora (*Greek*): Maiden. Corinne, Coralie, Corrie, Kora.

Courtney (*Old English*): Court dweller. Courteney, Courtnay, Kourtney.

Crystal (*Greek*): Ice. Christal, Chrystal, Crystel, Krystal.

Cynthia (*Latin*): From Cynthus. Cindi, Cindy, Cyn, Cyndy, Synthia.

Daisy (*Old English*): Eye of the day. Daisee, Daisey, Daisie.

Dale (*Old English*): Valley. Dayle, Daile.

Dana (*Old English*): From Denmark. Danna, Dayna.

Danielle Feminine form of Daniel (*Hebrew*): God is my Judge. Daniella, Danella, Dani, Daniela, Danny.

Darcie (*Irish*): Dark. Darcy, Darcee, Darsey.

Daria (*Greek*): Rich. Feminine form of Darius. Dari, Darice, Dorian.

Darryl (*Uncertain origin*; perhaps French place name). Daryl, Darrell.

Dawn (*Latin*): Modern replacement for Aurora meaning dawn. Dawna, Dawne, Dawnielle, Dawnn.

Deborah (*Hebrew*): Bee. Debra, Debbie, Debrah, Devora.

Deirdre (*Irish*): Fear, or raging woman. Deirdra, Dedra, Deidra, Dierdre.

Denise (*Greek*): Derived from "Dionysus," Greek god of wine. Deniece, Denny, Denyse, Denese, Denyce.

Diana (*Latin*): Divine. French form is Diane. Dyan, Diahann, Di, Dena.

Dinah (*Hebrew*): Justified. Dina, Dyna.

Dolores (*Spanish*): Sorrows. Delora, Deloria, Lola, Lolita.

Dominique Feminine form of Dominic (*Latin*): The lord. Dominica, Domini.

Donna (*Latin*): Lady. Dona, Donella, Donica, Donny.

Doreen (*Uncertain origin*): Dorene, Dorine, Doryne.

Doris Feminine form of Dorian (*Greek*): From Doris. Dori, Dorice, Dorrie.

Dorothy (*Greek*): Gift of God. Dolly, Dorrit, Dottie, Dorthy, Dorothe.

Earlene (*Old English*): Feminine form of Earl meaning noblemen or warrior. Earleen, Earline, Earlena.

Ebony (*Greek*): Dark wood. Ebbony, Eboney, Ebonyi, Eboni.

Eden (*Hebrew*): Delight; pleasure. Eaden, Edin.

Eileen Irish form of Helen (*Greek*): Light. Aileen, Ilene, Eilleen.

Elaine French form of Helen. Alaine, Elaina, Elane, Elayne.

Eleanor (*Uncertain origin*; possibly from Helen): Eleanora, Elinore, Ella, Elinor, Elly, Lenore, Leonora.

Elise French variation of Elizabeth (*Hebrew*): Oath of God. Elisa, Lise.

Ellen English form of Helen. Elen, Elena, Eleni, Ellie.

Elizabeth (*Hebrew*): Oath of God. Liza, Beth, Betsy, Betty, Elizabette, Eliza, Lisbeth, Elsa.

Eloise (*Uncertain origin*: perhaps from Louise): Aloysia, Heloise.

Emily (*Old German*): Industrious. Emeline, Emilia, Emmy, Milly.

Emma (*Old German*): Universal. Em, Ema, Emmie, Emmeline.

Emmanuelle Feminine form of Emanuel (*Hebrew*): God is with us. Emanuela.

Erica (*Scandinavian*): Ruler. Erika, Enrica, Ricki, Ricky, Rikki.

Erin (*Irish*): Ireland. Eirin, Erina, Erinn, Eryn.

Estelle (*Latin*): Star. Estella, Estrella, Estel, Stella, Stelle.

Esther (*Persian*): Star. Essie, Esta, Ester, Hester, Hetty.

Eugenie (*French*): Feminine form of Eugene (*Greek*): Well-born. Geena, Gena, Gina, Jeena.

Eve (*Hebrew*): Giver of life. Ava, Eva, Evie, Evita, Evy.

Evelyn (*Uncertain origin*; possibly *Old German*): Hazelnut. Eveline, Evelina, Evlin, Evlyn.

Faith (*Latin*): Trust; belief.

Fay (*Old French*): Fairy, or possibly a form of Faith. Faye, Fayth.

Felicia (*Latin*): Lucky. Felice, Felicity, Phelicia, Philicia.

Fern Plant name. Ferne.

Fleur (*French*): Flower. Fleurette, Fleurine.

Florence (*Latin*): To flower. Flor, Flora, Flore, Florrie, Floris, Flossie.

Frances Feminine form of Francis (*Latin*): From France. Francine, Franny.

Gabrielle Feminine form of Gabriel (*Hebrew*): Hero of God. Gabriella, Gabriele, Gabi, Gaby.

Gail Pet form of Abigail (*Hebrew*): A father's joy. Gayle, Gael, Gaylene.

Georgia Feminine form of George (*Greek*): Farmer. Georgiana, Georgine, Gina, Giorgia.

Gemma (*Italian*): Precious stone. Jemma.

Geraldine Feminine form of Gerald (*Old German*): Spear; ruler. Geralyn, Gerri, Deena, Jeraldine, Jeri.

Germaine (*French*): From Germany. Germain, Jermain, Jermaine, Jermayn.

Ghaliya (*Arabic*): Sweet smelling.

Gillian English form of Juliana (*Latin*): Youthful. Gillianne, Gillie, Jillian.

Giselle (*Old German*): Pledge; hostage. Gisella, Gizella, Giza.

Glenna Feminine form of Glen (*Irish*): Glen, valley. Glenda, Glenn, Gleneen.

Gloria (*Latin*): Glory. Glorie, Gloriana, Gloris, Glori.

Glynis (*Welsh*): Valley, and (*Scottish*): Glen. Glynnis, Glinys, Glynes.

Gretchen (*Greek*): Pearl. German form of Margaret.

Gwendolyn (*Welsh*): Fair; blessed. Gwendolen, Gwenith, Gwendolynne.

Habibah (*Arabic*): Loved one.

Hannah (*Hebrew*): Grace. Related to Anna, Ann, Anne.

Harriet Feminine form of Harry (*Old German*): Ruler of home. Harriett, Harriette, Harriot, Harrietta, Hattie.

Harmony (*Latin*): Harmony. Harmonie.

Hayley (*Old English*): High meadow. Hailey, Halie, Haylee.

Heather (*English*): Plant name.

Heidi (*German*): Pet form of Adelaide. Heide.

Helen (*Greek*): Light. Helana, Hellene, Aileen, Elaine, Elinor, Lenore, Nellie.

Hilary (*Latin*): Cheerful. Hillary, Hillery, Hilairie, Alaire.

Hollis (*Old English*): Place name. Near the holly bushes.

Holly Plant name. Hollie, Holli.

Honor (*Latin*): Integrity. Honora, Honnor, Honnour, Honnoure.

Hope (*Old English*): Expectation; belief.

Ingrid (*Scandinavian*): Beautiful. Inga, Inge, Ingmar.

Irene (*Greek*): Peace. Arina, Eireen, Irina, Rene, Rina.

Isabel (*Hebrew*): God's oath. Spanish/Portuguese variation of Elizabeth. Belle, Isabella, Isabelle, Isobell.

Ivana Feminine form of Slavic form of John (*Hebrew*): God is gracious. Ivanna, Iva.

Jacqueline (*French*): Feminine diminutive of Jacques (*Hebrew*):
Supplanting; following after. Jacquelyne, Jaclyn, Jackie,
Jaquette, Jacqui.

Jade Jewel name. Jayde.

Jamie (*Scottish*): Diminutive form of James (*Hebrew*):
Supplanting; following after. Jaime, Jaimie, Jayme, Jaymie.

Jamila (*Arabic*): Lovely. Jamilah, Jamilla, Jamille.

Jane Feminine form of John (*Hebrew*): God
is gracious. Jayne, Jana, Janella, Janey,
Janis.

Janet Diminutive form of Jane. Janeta,
Janetta, Janette, Jennetta.

Janice Variation of Jane. Janis, Jannice,
Janyce.

Jasmine (*Arabic*): Plant name. Jasmin,
Jasmina, Yasmeen, Yasmin, Yasmine.

Jean (*Scottish*): Form of Jane. Jeanne,
Jeana, Jeanelle, Jeannine, Jeanie,
Jennetta, Jennine.

Jena (*Arabic*): Little bird. Jenna.

Jennifer (*Welsh*): White and soft. Jen, Jenifer, Jennie, Jenny,
Gennifer.

Jessica (*Hebrew*): He beholds. Jess, Jesse, Jesseca, Jessie.

Jill Diminutive of Gillian (*Latin*): Youthful. Jillian, Jilly.

Joan Feminine form of John (*Hebrew*): God is gracious. Joani, Joni, Joanne.

Joanna Variation of Jane or Joan. Jo, Joann, Jo Ann, Johannah.

Jocelyn (*Old German*): Tribal name. Jocelin, Joselyn, Josselyn, Joycelin.

Jodie Diminutive form of Judith (*Hebrew*): Object of praise. Jodi, Jody.

Joelle Feminine form of Joel (*Hebrew*): Jehovah is the Lord. Joela, Joella, Joellen.

Jolie (*French*): Pretty. Jolee, Joley, Joli, Joly.

Joy The word used as a name. Joie, Joye, Joi, Joya.

Joyce (*Latin*): Merry; joyful. Joyce, Joyse.

Judith (*Hebrew*): Jewess. Juddi, Judie, Judy.

Julia Feminine form of Julius (*Latin*): Downy hair. Julie, Juliette, Juliana.

June Name of the month.

Justine (*Latin*): Fair; righteous. Originally Justina from the masculine, Justin. Justene, Justina.

Kali (*Sanskrit*): Energy.

Kalila (*Arabic*): Beloved. Kailey, Kaly, Kylila.

Kamilah (*Arabic*): Perfect. Kamila, Kamilla, Kamillah.

Karen (*Greek*): Pure. Danish variation of Katherine (*Greek*). Caryn, Caren, Caron, Karon, Karyn.

Katherine (*Greek*): Pure. Kathryn, Katrina, Kate, Katie, Kathleen, Kathy, Kay.

Kayla (*Hebrew*): Crown; laurel. Kaela, Kaylyn, Kaila.

Keisha (*Modern name*): Variation of Lakeisha, variation of Aisha (*Arabic*): Woman.

Kelly (*Irish*): Warrior. Kealey, Kayley, Keely, Kiley, Kelley, Keilly.

Kelsey (*Old English*): Place name. Kelcey, Kelcy, Kelsy.

Kendra (*Uncertain origin; possible combination of Ken and Sandra*): Kenna, Kinna.

Kerry (*Irish*): Place name, also dark. Kerri, Keri, Kerrie, Keree, Kerrey.

Kimberly (*Old English*): Place name. Kim, Kimberley, Kimbra.

Kirsten Scandinavian variation of Christine (*Greek*): Christian. Kersten, Keirstan, Kirstin, Kirstyn.

Kristin Combination of Kirsten and Kristin; variation of Christine. Kristan, Krista, Kristel, Krissie.

Kyle (*Scottish*): Narrow piece of land.

Ladonna Modern name combining La– with Donna.

Lakeisha (*Arabic*): Woman. Modern name combining La– with Aisha or Aiesha. Lakeesha, Lakeysha, Keisha.

Larissa (*Latin*): Cheerful; light-hearted. Laryssa, Lissa, Lyssa.

Lashanna Modern name combining La– with Shannon. Lashannon, Lashauna.

Latanya Modern name combining La– with Tanya. Latania, Latonia, Latonya.

Latoya Modern name with La– prefix. Latoyla.

Latrice Modern name combining La– with Patricia (*Latin*): Noble. Latrecia, Latreece, Latreshia.

Laura (*Latin*): Laurel or bay tree. Lora, Lori, Laurel, Lorette, Lorraine.

Lauren (*Latin*): Laurel or bay tree. Laureen, Loreen, Loren, Lurene.

Leila (*Arabic*): Night. Layla, Leilah, Lelah, Lila.

Lesley (*Scottish*): Place name. Lesli, Lesly, Lesslie, Leslye.

Letitia (*Latin*): Gladness. Latisha, Latashia, Letisha, Letice, Letty, Tisha.

Levanna (*Hebrew*): Shining white, or the moon. Levana, Lewanna, Livana.

Liberty Word used as a name.

A New Baby, A New Name

Inventing a name is a complement to life's most creative act, giving birth. Try making an anagram by switching the letters of a word or name to make an original name. For example, "earth" becomes *Retha*. Or create a name from parts of the parents' names. Thus, (Deb)orah and (Ron)ald's child could be *Debron*. Create a new name from a famous name by using its parts, as in *Elsley* from (El)vis Pre(sley). Drop a first syllable to invent a name like *Ariana* from Mariana; or eliminate a last syllable to make *Aman* from Amanda. Invert the syllables of a name for a whole new sound, like *Ronsha* from Sharon. There really are no rules, just imaginative choices.

Linda (*Spanish*): Pretty. Lynda, Lynn, Lindy, Linn, Lynnda.

Lindsay (*Scottish*): Place name. Lindsey, Lyndsey, Lynsey, Lindsie, Lynsie.

Lisa Diminutive of Elizabeth (*Hebrew*): Oath of God. Lise, Liza.

Lois Variation of Louise (*Old German*): Warrior.

Louise (*Old German*): Warrior. Feminine form of Louis. Louisa, Heloise, Lola.

Luana (*Old German*): Combined name of Louise and Anne. Lewanna, Luwana, Louanne.

Lucy (*Latin*): Light. Lucille, Lucinda, Lucia.

Lydia (*Greek*): From Lydia. Lidia, Lydie.

Madeline (*Greek*): From Magdala. Madeleine, Madalyn, Madelene, Madalyn, Madelynne, Mady, Maudlin, Maude.

Mallory (*Old French*): Unlucky. Malory, Malloreigh, Mallorie, Malorey.

Mandy (*Latin*): Much loved. Pet form of Amanda or Miranda. Mandie, Mandee.

Marcia Feminine form of Marcus (*Latin*): Martial. Marcie, Marcy, Marsha.

Margaret (*Greek*): Pearl. Greta, Marjorie, Margeret, Margy, Meg, Peggy, Rita.

Maria Variation of Mary. Greek version of Miriam (*Hebrew*): Bitter. (*French*): Mariah.

Marianne Combination of Marie (*Hebrew*): Bitter, and Ann (*Hebrew*): Grace. Mariane, Marianna, Maryanna.

Mariel Dutch and French version of Mary (*Hebrew*): Bitter. Marella, Mariela, Marielle.

Marissa (*Latin*): Of the sea. Form of Maris. Maresa, Marisse, Merissa.

Mary Greek version of Miriam (*Hebrew*): Bitter.

Maxine Feminine form of Max (*Latin*): Greatest. Maxene, Maxeen, Maxina.

Megan (*Welsh*): Diminutive of Margaret. Meagan, Meaghan, Meg, Meghan.

Melanie (*Greek*): Dark. Melani, Melaney, Melane, Melaine, Melony.

Melinda (*Latin*): Honey. Malinda, Melynda, Mindy, Melynda.

Melissa (*Greek*): Bee. Lissa, Missy, Mellissa, Melisa, Mellisa.

Meredith (*Old Welsh*): Great ruler. Meridith, Meredithe.

Meriel Variation of Muriel (*Irish*): Sea-bright. Meryl, Merial, Meriol.

Merry (*Old English*): Lighthearted. Merri, Merrili, Merrielle.

Mia (*Italian*): Mine.

Michelle (*French*): Feminine form of Michael (*Hebrew*): Who is like the Lord? Mechelle, Michele, Michell, Micki.

Millicent (*Old German*): Noble strength. Melisande, Milicent, Millisent, Millie.

Mirabel (*Latin*): Wonderful. Mira, Mirabella, Mirabelle.

Miranda (*Latin*): Admirable. Mandy, Mandi, Mira, Myranda, Randi, Randy.

Miriam (*Hebrew*): Bitter, or rebellious. Mariam, Miryam, Mimi.

Molly Pet name for Mary (*Hebrew*): Bitter. Mollie, Molley.

Monica (*Greek*): Alone, or (*Latin*): Adviser. Monika, Monique, Mona.

Morgan (*Welsh*): Great; bright. Morganna, Morgen, Morganne.

Muriel (*Irish*): Sea-bright. Murial, Murielle.

Nadine French form of Nadia (*Russian*): Hope. Nadeen, Nadene, Naydeen.

Nancy French form of Ann (*Hebrew*): Grace. Nance, Nanette, Nancie, Nan.

Naomi (*Hebrew*): Pleasantness; delight. Naoma, Noemi, Naomie.

Natalie (*Latin*): Birthday of the Lord. Natelie, Natalia, Natalee.

Natasha Russian version of Natalie. Nastaliya, Natascha.

Nell Pet form of Eleanor (*Greek*): Bright one. Nel, Nellie, Nelly, Nelley.

Nicole (*Greek*): Victory of the people. Feminine form of Nicholas. Nicolette, Nicki, Niki.

Nina (*Spanish*): Little girl. Variation of Ann (*Hebrew*): Grace. Neena.

Noelle (*French*): Christmas. Noela, Noelleen, Noeline, Noleen.

Olga (*Russian*): Holy. Elga, Helga, Ola, Olia.

Olivia (*Latin*): Olive tree. Liv, Liva, Livvie, Livy, Olive, Olivette.

Olympia (*Greek*): From Mount Olympus.

Opal Jewel name. Opalina, Opaline.

Oriana (*Latin*): Dawn; sunrise. Oria, Oriane, Orianna.

Page (*French*): Surname in Middle Ages for assistant to a knight. Paige.

Pamela (*Greek*): All honey. Pam, Pamala, Pamella, Pamila, Pammala.

Patience Word used as a name.

Patricia (*Latin*): Noble; patrician. Patrice, Patti, Tricia, Trisha.

Paula Feminine form of Paul (*Latin*): Small. Paola, Pauline, Pauletta, Polly.

Peggy Diminutive of Margaret (*Latin*): Pearl. Peg, Pegeen, Peggie.

Penelope (*Greek*): Weaver. Pennelope, Penny, Pen, Pennie.

Phaedra (*Greek*): Bright. Phedra, Faydra.

Phoebe (*Greek*): Pure; bright. Phebe, Phoebey.

Phyllis (*Greek*): Leafy branch. Phylis, Phillis, Phylliss.

Pia (*Latin*): Pious.

Polly Variation of Molly. Diminutive form of Mary (*Hebrew*): Bitter.

Priscilla (*Latin*): Ancient. Cilla, Priscella, Prisilla.

Prudence (*Latin*): Caution. Prue, Prudy, Prudie.

Quiana Modern form of Anna. Quianna, Kiana.

Rachel (*Hebrew*): Ewe. Rachael, Rachele, Rachil, Raquel, Rashell, Rae.

Raina Variation of Regina (*Latin*): Queen. Rainah, Rayna, Raynelle.

Randy Pet form of Miranda (*Latin*): Admirable. Randee, Randi.

Rani (*Sanskrit*): Queen. Raine, Rana, Rayna, Raynell.

Rashida (*Turkish*): Righteous. Rasheeda, Rashidah.

Rebecca (*Hebrew*): Joined; tied. Becky, Bekka, Reba, Rebekah.

Regan (*Irish*): Descendant of a small ruler. Form of Regina.

Regina (*Latin*): Queen. Reggie, Regine, Reine, Reyna.

Rhea (*Greek*): Earth. Rea, Rhia, Ria.

Roberta Feminine form of Robert (*Old English*): Bright; fame. Berta, Bertie, Bobbie.

Robin Diminutive form of Robert. Robyn, Robbie.

Rohana (*Sanskrit*): Sandalwood. Rohanna.

Rosalind (*Spanish*): Pretty rose. Rosaline, Rosalynn, Rozelle, Roselinda.

Initial Instructions

It's no surprise that someone with the initials HAG would rather not have a monogram on her sweater. The little things in life that adults find merely annoying can bring on a case of acute mortification in a child. The second grader whose classmates discover that his initials spell *DOG* or *PIG* is not likely to forgive his parents in a hurry. So it's wise to pay attention to how the first letters of each name relate to each other when they stand alone. If the middle name you've chosen is Owen, and your last name is Grant, don't set your heart on David (DOG), or Lawrence (LOG), or, especially, Howard (HOG).

Rose (*Latin*): Flower name. Rosie, Rosalie, Rosanna, Rosella, Rosy.

Ronni Feminine form of Ronald (*Old English*): Strong counsel. Roni, Ronee, Ronny, Ronette.

Roxanne (*Persian*): Dawn. Roxana, Roxane, Roxie, Roxy.

Ruth (*Hebrew*): Companion; friend. Ruthy, Ruthella, Ruthe, Ruthie.

Sabrina (*Latin*): Place name. Sabryna, Sabreena, Brina.

Sally Diminutive of Sarah (*Hebrew*): Princess. Salli, Sallie, Sal, Sallyanne.

Samantha Feminine form of Samuel (*Hebrew*): Told by God. Sam, Semantha, Sammantha.

Sandra Diminutive of Alexandra (*Greek*): Defender of man. Sandy, Sondra, Sohndra, Zandra.

Sarah (*Hebrew*): Princess. Sara, Sadie, Sari, Shara, Zara.

Selina (*Greek*): Moon goddess. Selena, Salina, Salena, Celina, Cellina.

Serena (*Latin*): Calm; tranquil. Sereena, Serenah, Serenna, Serina.

Shafaye Modern combination of Sha– and Faye. Other names using Sha– prefix: Shalaya, Shalonda, Shaketa, Shameka, Shameta, Sherena.

Shan Phonetic spelling of Sian, the Welsh form of Jane. Shannay, Shaneen, Shanelle. Used as a prefix in: Shanecka, Shanetta, Shanika, Shanita, Shannell, Shanta, Shantrice.

Shannon (*Irish*): Ancient or old one. Shannan, Shauna, Shawna, Shanna, Shana.

Shaneika Modern combination with Sha– prefix. Shaneikah, Shanika, Shaneyka.

Shanelle Modern phonetic spelling of Chanel. Shanel, Shanella, Shannel, Shenelle.

Sharon (*Hebrew*): The plain. Shari, Sherri, Sharonda, Sharan, Sharen, Sharene, Sharin.

Shavonne Phonetic spelling of Siobhan, Irish variation of Joan. Feminine form of John (*Hebrew*): The Lord is gracious. Shevon, Shivonne, Shevonne.

Shawn Phonetic spelling of Sean (*Irish*). Variation of John. Shaun, Shauna, Shawna, Shona.

Sheena Irish variation of Jane. Feminine form of John. Sheenah, Shena, Sheona, Shiona.

Sheila Irish variation of Celia (*Latin*): Blind. Sheela, Sheelah, Sheilah, Shelagh.

Shelby (*Old English*): Land on the edge. Shelbey, Shellby.

Shelley (Old English): Meadow on the slope. Shellie, Shelly, Shelli.

Sophia (*Greek*): Wisdom. Sofia, Sofie, Sonia, Sophy, Zofia.

Stacey Diminutive of Anastasia (*Greek*): Resurrection. Stacy, Stacie, Staci.

Stephanie Feminine form of Stephen (*Greek*): Crown. Stefanie, Stefani, Stephenie, Stephannie, Steffi.

Susan (*Hebrew*): Lily. Susannah, Susanne, Susie, Suzy, Sue.

Sybil (*Greek*): Seer; prophetess. Sibyl, Cybill, Sibelle.

Sydney Place name. Sydnie.

Tabitha (*Aramaic*): Gazelle. Tabatha, Tabetha, Tabbey, Tabbi.

Tahira (*Arabic*): Virginal; pure.

Tamara (*Hebrew*): Palm tree. Tamra, Tamyra, Tamar, Tamarra, Tammy.

Who hath not owned, with rapture-smitten frame, The power of grace, the magic of a name?

THOMAS CAMPBELL

Tamika Modern name of uncertain origin. Tameeka, Tamieka, Tamike.

Tanisha Modern name, possibly combining Ta– and Aisha (*Arabic*): Woman. Taneesha, Tanesha, Teneisha.

Tanya (*Russian*): Fairy queen, or (*Greek*): Sun. Tannia, Tana, Tahnya.

Tara (*Irish*): Rocky hill. Tarah, Tarra, Tarrah.

Taylor (*Middle English*): Occupational name. Tailor, Tayler.

Theresa (*Greek*): Harvest. Teresa, Terese, Terri, Terry, Teressa, Tresa, Tess.

Tiffany (*Greek*): Manifestation of God. Tifani, Tiffney, Tiffini, Tiffiny.

Tracy Diminutive of Theresa (*Greek*): Harvest. Tracey, Tracie, Traci.

Trudy Diminutive of Gertrude (*Old English*): Strength. Trudie.

Tuesday Day name used as first name.

Tyne (*English*): River. Tyna.

Ulima (*Arabic*): Wise. Ullima.

Unity (*Middle English*): Oneness. Unita.

Ursula (*Latin*): Little female bear. Ursa, Ursala, Ursella.

Valentine (*Latin*): To be strong. Teena, Tina, Val, Valena.

Valerie (*Latin*): Strong. Val, Valeria, Valery.

Vanessa (*Greek*): Butterfly. Vanesse, Vanna, Vanni, Nessa.

Vera (*Latin*): Truth. Vere, Verina, Verine, Veria.

Veronica (*Latin*): True image. Ronnie, Ronica, Veronika, Veronique.

Victoria Feminine form of Victor (*Latin*): Victory. Vicky, Vicki, Vikki, Tori.

Virginia (*Latin*): Maiden. Ginger, Ginny, Jinney, Virginie.

Vivian (*Latin*): Alive. Vivien, Vivienne.

Wanda Slavic tribal name, or (*Old English*): Wanderer. Wennda, Wandie.

Wendy Literary name from Peter Pan. Wendee, Wendi, Wendie.

Whitney (*Old English*): White island. Whitnee, Whitnie, Whitny.

Winona (*Sioux*): First born daughter. Wenona, Wenonah, Winnie, Winonah.

Xaviera Feminine form of Xavier (*Basque*): New house. Zaviera.

Yasmin (*Arabic*): Plant name. Yasmine, Yasmeena, Jasmine.

Yolanda (*Greek*): Violet flower. Yolande, Jolanna, Iolande.

Yvonne Feminine form of Ivo (*Old German*): Yew wood, or archer. Yvone, Evonne, Yvette.

Zahra (*Arabic*): White. Zahrah.

Zena Variation of Xenia (*Greek*): Welcoming. Zina.

Zoe (*Greek*): Life.

Introducing...!

A birth announcement could quite possibly be the best news the mail carries. Store bought, printed, or original, yours should proclaim your baby's name, date of birth, weight, and parents' names. Any motif that suits your fancy is a good one. Teddy bears and balloons, ribbons and bows, pink and blue, are all adorable adornments. There are novelties, too: an ice cream cone for your "latest scoop," a tax form for your new "deduction," a star for "a star is born." Or bring in the whole family: Draw a family chart highlighting the baby's name, or have brothers and sisters introduce their new sibling. Make your announcement a celebration.

It's in the Stars

Astrology has its believers and detractors, but almost everyone is seduced by the system's possibilities for truth-telling. The zodiac, according to ancient astrologists, cites the position of the sun and planets in relation to twelve zodiac "signs" named for constellations. The theory holds that being born under a certain sign influences personality. So watch your baby and see if these traits apply.

Aries	Mar. 21–Apr. 19	Ram	Bold, courageous, energetic
Taurus	Apr. 20–May 20	Bull	Conservative, possessive, loyal
Gemini	May 21–June 20	Twins	Lively, talkative, intelligent
Cancer	June 21–July 22	Crab	Emotional, patriotic, home loving
Leo	July 23–Aug. 22	Lion	Cheerful, proud, powerful
Virgo	Aug. 23–Sept. 22	Virgin	Modest, practical, tidy
Libra	Sept. 23–Oct. 22	Scales	Companionable, diplomatic, pleasant
Scorpio	Oct. 24–Nov. 21	Scorpion	Secretive, intense, passionate
Sagittarius	Nov. 22–Dec. 21	Archer	Cheerful, generous, restless
Capricorn	Dec. 22–Jan. 19	Goat	Ambitious, cautious, practical
Aquarius	Jan. 20–Feb. 18	Water Bearer	Curious, outgoing, indepedent
Pisces	Feb. 19–Mar. 20	Fish	Artistic, emotional, sensitive

Boys' Names

Aaron (*Hebrew*): High mountain, or to shine. Aran, Aharon, Arin.

Abdul (*Arabic*): Servant of. Abdullah.

Abraham (*Hebrew*): Father of the multitude. Abram, Ibrahim, Avram.

Adair (*Scottish*): Oak tree ford. Adaire, Adare.

Adam (*Hebrew*): Red earth. Addam, Adhamh.

Ahsan (*Arabic*): Compassion.

Aidan (*Irish*): Fire. Aden, Aiden.

Alan (*Irish*): Rock, or noble. Allen, Allan.

Albert (*Old German*): Noble; brilliant. Albie, Bert.

Alexander (*Greek*): Defender of men. Alec, Alexi, Sandor.

Ali (*Arabic*): The exalted one.

Alfred (*Old English*): Elf counsel. Alf, Alfredo, Alfy, Fred.

Andrew (*Greek*): Manly. Andre, Andro, Drew.

Anthony (*Latin*): Beyond price, or (*Greek*): Flower. Antony, Tony.

Arlen (*Irish*): Pledge, oath. Arlan, Arlin, Arlyn.

Ashton (*Old English*): Place name. Ash tree farm.

Avery (*Old English*): Elf ruler. Averey.

Barry (*Irish*): Sharp; spear. Bari, Barrie.

Bart Diminutive of Bartholomew (*Aramaic*): Son of Talmai. Bartlett.

Benjamin (*Hebrew*): Son of my right hand. Benjamen, Ben, Benji.

Bernard (*Old German*): Bear; courageous. Barnard, Barney, Bern.

Bertram (*Old German*): Bright raven. Bartram, Berton.

Brandon (*Old English*): Place name. Broom-covered hill. Variation of Brendan. Brandin, Brannon.

Bradley (*Old English*): Broad meadow. Brad, Lee.

Brendan (*Irish*): Smelly hair. Brendon, Brennan.

Brent (*Old English*): Place name. High place or burnt. Brentan.

Brett (*Latin*): Man from Britain. Bret, Bretton.

Brian (*Irish*): Strong. Bryant, Bryon.

Broderick (*Old Norse*): Brother. Broderic, Brod, Rick, Ricky.

Bruce (*Old French*): From the wood thicket. Brucie.

Bryce (*Uncertain origin*): Bryce.

Burton (*Old English*): Fortified enclosure. Bert, Burt.

Calvin (*Latin*): Hairless. Cal, Kalvin.

Cameron (*Scottish*): Crooked nose. Cam, Camron.

Campbell (*Scottish*): Crooked mouth.

Carl German variation of Charles (*Old English*): Man.

Carleton (*Old English*): Farmer's town. Carlton, Charlton.

Carter (*Old English*): One who drives carts.

Chad (*Old English*): Uncertain meaning.

Chandler (*Old French*): Candle merchant.

Charles (*Old German*): Man. Carel, Charley, Carroll, Karl.

Christian (*Greek*): Bearer of Christ. Chris, Kit, Kristofer.

Clark (*Old French*): Clerk; scholar. Clarke.

Clayton (*Old English*): Living near clay. Clay.

Clifford (*Old English*): Crossing near a cliff. Cliff.

Clinton (*Old English*): Settlement near a hill. Clint.

Cody (*Old English*): Pillow; cushion. Codie, Kody.

Cole Diminutive for Nicholas (*Greek*): People of victory.

Colin (*Irish*): Youth. Colan, Collin.

Connor (*Irish*): High desire. Conor.

Conrad (*Old German):* Courageous advice. Con, Connie, Konrad, Curt, Kurt.

Corey (*Irish*): Place name. The hollow. Cory, Corrie, Corry, Korie.

Craig (*Irish*): Rock.

Curtis (*Old French*): Courteous. Curt, Curtiss, Kurtis.

Dale (*Old English*): Valley. Dayle, Dael.

Damian (*Greek*): To tame. Damien, Damion, Damon.

If your name is to live at all, it is so much more to have it live in people's hearts than only in their brains!

OLIVER WENDELL HOLMES

Daniel (*Hebrew*): God is my judge. Dan, Danny, Daniele.

Darryl (*French*): Place name. Darell, Daryl, Deryl.

Darren (*Irish*): Great. Daren, Darin, Darryn.

David (*Hebrew*): Beloved. Dave, Davis, Davy.

Dean (*Old English*): Valley, or church official. Deane, Dene.

Demetrius (*Greek*): Follower of Demeter. Demetri, Dimitri, Dimitrios.

Dennis (*Greek*): Follower of Dionysus. Den, Denny, Denis.

Derek (*Old German*): Ruler of the people. Derreck, Derrek, Derk, Dirk.

Devlin (*Irish*): Fierce courage. Devland, Devlen, Devlyn.

Dominic (*Latin*): The lord. Dominick, Dom, Nick.

Donald (*Irish*): World ruler. Donal, Donny, Don.

Donovan (*Irish*): Dark brown. Donavon, Donoven.

Dorian (*Greek*): From Doris. Doren, Dorrian.

Douglas (*Scottish*): Dark water. Doug, Douglass.

Drew Diminutive of Andrew (*Greek*): Manly.

Dustin (*Old German*): Brave warrior. Dusty, Dust.

Dwayne (*Irish*): Swarthy. Duane, Dwaine, Duwayne.

Dylan (*Welsh*): Son of the waves. Name of legendary sea god.

Earl (*Old English*): Nobleman; leader. Earle, Errol.

Edgar (*Old English*): Spear; prosperity. Ed.

Edmund (*Old English*): Wealthy protector. Edmond, Ed, Ned.

Edward (*Old English*): Wealthy defender. Ed, Eddie, Ted.

Edwin (*Old English*): Wealthy friend. Edwyn, Eddy, Teddy.

Eli (*Hebrew*): On high. Elie, Ely.

Elijah (*Hebrew*): The Lord is God. Eli, Elias, Elihu.

Elliot (*English*): Form of Eli or Elijah. Elliott, Eliott.

Elton (*Old English*): Ella's town. Eldon, Ellton.

Emanuel (*Hebrew*): God is with us. Emmanuel, Eman, Manny.

Emil (*Old German*): Eager. Emile, Emlen.

Emmett (*Uncertain origin; possibly Old German*): Energetic.

Ephraim (*Hebrew*): Fruitful. Efraim, Efrem, Ephrem.

Eric (*Scandinavian*): Ruler. Erich, Erick, Rick.

Ernest (*German*): Earnestness. Earnest, Ernie, Ernst.

Ethan (*Hebrew*): Constancy. Etan.

Eugene (*Greek*): Well-born. Gene.

Names That Follow Footsteps

What inspires a baby's name? Naming a baby after a relative keeps the family history alive. A mother's maiden name, if it accompanies the surname without a great clash, preserves both parents' heritages. A famous person's name—John Kennedy, for example—honors a memory. Names inspired by an ethnic background, like Scandinavian Hans and Irish Kelly, are a link between the past and the future. Of course, a parent's name is the most direct source, although few children are actually called by that name; to avoid confusion, boys named after fathers named Robert are usually called Bob and girls named after mothers named Margaret typically become Peggy. So sometimes a name's significance may be more important than its use.

Evan Welsh form of John (*Hebrew*): God is Gracious. Even, Evans.

Everett English form of Everard (*Old German*): Boar; hard. Everet.

Ezra (*Hebrew*): Help. Esra, Azariah, Ezer.

Farley (*Old English*): Meadow of the sheep. Farleigh, Farrley.

Fletcher (*Middle English*): Arrow maker. Fletch.

Floyd (*Welsh*): Gray, or (*Irish*): Will of God.

Francis (*Latin*): Frenchman. Franco, Fran, Franko, Frans, Francesco.

Frank Diminutive of Francis or Franklin.

Franklin (*Middle English*): Free landholder. Francklin, Franklyn.

Frederick (*Old German*): Peaceful ruler. Frederic, Eric, Fritz.

Gabriel (*Hebrew*): Hero of God. Gabe, Gabi, Gabriele.

Galen (*Greek*): Healer, or calm. Gaelen, Gaylon, Galin.

Gannon (*Irish*): Fair-skinned.

Gardner (*Middle English*): Gardener. Gardener, Gardiner.

Garrett Variation of Gerard (*Old German*): Spear; brave. Jarrett.

Garth (*Scandinavian*): Keeper of the garden.

Gary Likely taken from Garrett, a form of Gerard (*Old German*): Spear. Garry, Garrie.

Gavin Form of Gawain (*Welsh*): White hawk. Gavan, Gaven, Gavyn.

Gaylord (*Old French*): Lively; high-spirited. Gayelord, Gaylor.

Geoffrey (*Old German*): Peace; an unclear element. Geoffery, Jeffery, Jeffrey.

George (*Greek*): Farmer. Georges, Giorgio.

Gerald (*Old German*): Spear; ruler. Gerrald, Jerold, Gerry, Jerry.

Gerard (*Old German*): Spear; brave. Garrard, Gerry.

Gideon (*Hebrew*): Feller of trees. Gideone.

Gilbert (*Old German*): Pledge; bright. Gilberto, Bert, Burt.

Giles (*Greek*): Young goat. Gilles, Gyles.

Glen (*Irish*): Place name; glen. Glenn, Glynn.

Gordon (*Scottish*): Clan name. Gordan, Gorden, Gordie.

Graham (*Scottish*): Clan name. Grahame, Graeme.

Granger (*French*): Farmer.

Grant (*French*): Tall; big.

Gregory (*Greek*): Watchful. Greggory, Greg, Gregg.

Griffin (*Latin*): Mythological animal, half eagle and lion. Griffon.

Gunther (*Scandinavian*): Warrior. Gunter, Gunthar.

Guthrie (*Irish*): Windy spot.

Guy (*Uncertain origin*): Guido.

Hakeem (*Arabic*): Wise; all-knowing. Hakim.

Hamilton (*Old English*): Place name. Hamill.

Hans Scandinavian form of John (*Hebrew*): God is gracious.

Harlan (*Old German*): Army land. Harland, Harlen, Harlin.

Harold (*Old English*): Army power. Hal, Harald, Harry, Herrick.

Harper (*Old English*): Harp player.

Harrison (*Old English*): Son of Harry. Harris.

Harvey (*Old French*): Strong; ardent. Herve, Harve, Harvy.

Hashim (*Arabic*): Crusher of evil. Hasheem.

Hassan (*Arabic*): Handsome. Hasan.

Henry (*Old German*): Home ruler. Enrico, Heinrich, Hank, Henrique.

Herbert (*Old German*): Bright; army. Bert, Hebert, Herb.

Herman (*Old German*): Man of the army. Armand, Ermin, Hermann.

Heywood (*Old English*): Place name. Hedged forest. Haywood, Woody.

Hobart American form of Hubert (*Old German*).

Holden (*Old English*): Place name. Hollow valley.

Howard (*Old English*): Uncertain meaning. Howie.

Hubert (*Old German*): Bright intellect. Bert, Hobart, Huberto, Hubie.

Hugh (*Old German*): Mind; soul. Hughes, Huey.

Humphrey (*Old German*): Uncertain meaning. Humphery, Humphry.

Hunter (*Old English*): Hunter. Occupational name.

Hussein (*Arabic*): Small handsome one.

One of the few, the immortal names,
That were not born to die.

FITZ-GREENE HALLECK

Ian Scottish form of John (*Hebrew*): God is gracious.

Irving (*Scottish*): Place name. Ervin, Irvine, Irv.

Isaac (*Hebrew*): Laughter. Ike, Itzak, Izaak, Yitzhak.

Ivan Russian form of John.

Jack Pet form of John. Jacky, Jackie.

Jackson (*Old English*): Son of Jack.

Jacob (*Hebrew*): He who supplants. Jakob, Jakov, Jake, Jack.

Jamal (*Arabic*): Handsome. Jamaal, Jamill, Jammal.

James English form of Jacob (*Hebrew*): He who supplants. Jim, Jimmy.

Jared (*Hebrew*): He descends. Jarad, Jerad, Jerrad.

Jason From Joshua (*Hebrew*): The Lord is salvation. Jayson, Jase.

Jay (*Latin*): Jaybird; chatterer. Jaye.

Jed Pet form of Jedidiah (*Hebrew*): Beloved of the Lord.

Jefferson (*Old English*): Son of Jeffrey. Jeff.

Jeffrey (*Old German*): Peace; an unclear element. Geoffrey, Godfrey, Jeffery.

Jeremy Modern form of Jeremiah (*Hebrew*): The Lord exalts. Jeramie, Jereme, Jerry.

Jermaine (*Latin*): From Germany. Jermainn, Jermane.

Jerome (*Greek*): Sacred name. Gerome, Jerrome, Jerry.

Jesse (*Hebrew*): God exists. Jess, Jessie.

Joel (*Hebrew*): Jehovah is the Lord.

John (*Hebrew*): The Lord is gracious. Hans, Ivan, Jack, Jan, Seann, Vanya, Yanni, Zane.

Jonah (*Hebrew*): Dove. Jonas.

Jonathan Gift of God. Jon, Jonathon, Johnathan.

Jordan (*Hebrew*): To descend. Jourdan, Jory, Jordon.

Joseph (*Hebrew*): God increases. Joe, Jose, Jozef, Jody.

Joshua (*Hebrew*): The Lord is salvation. Josh.

Julian Variation of Julius (*Latin*): Downy hair. Julien.

Julius (*Latin*): Downy hair. Also clan name. Giulo, Jule, Jules, Julio.

Justin (*Latin*): Just; righteous. Justus, Justyn.

Kamal (*Arabic*): Perfection. Kameel, Kamil.

Kareem (*Arabic*): Highborn; generous. Karim.

Karl Form of Charles (*Old German*): Man. Karel, Karol.

Kedar (*Arabic*): Powerful. Kadar.

Keenan (*Irish*): Small and ancient. Keen, Kienan, Kienen.

Keith (*Scottish*): Wood.

Keir (*Irish*): Swarthy.

Kendall (*Old English*): Place name. Valley of the river Kent. Kendal, Kendell.

Kenneth (*Irish*): Fair one. Ken, Kennet, Kenny.

Kent (*Old English*): Place name.

Kevin (*Irish*): Handsome. Kevan, Kevon.

Kimball (*Old English*): Warrior chief. Kim, Kimbell.

Kirk (*Old Norse*): Church. Kerk.

Kurt Diminutive of Konrad (*Old German*): Brave counsel. Conrad, Curt.

Kyle (*Irish*): Narrow piece of land.

Laban (*Hebrew*): White.

Lamar (*Old German*): Land famous. Lemar.

Lambert (*Old German*): Land brilliant. Bert, Lamberto.

Lance Variation of Lancelot (*Old English*): Servant.

Lane (*Middle English*): Place name. Layne.

Lawrence (*Latin*): From Laurentium. Laurence, Lorin, Larry, Lonny.

Lee (*Old English*): Place name. Pasture or meadow. Leigh.

Leland (*Old English*): Place name. Leighland, Leyland.

Leo (*Latin*): Lion.

Leon (*Greek*): Form of Leo.

Leonard (*Old German*): Strong as a lion. Len, Lenny, Leonardo, Lonny.

Leroy (*Old French*): The king. Elroi, Elroy, Lee, Leroi, Roy.

Leslie (*Scottish*): Place name. Lesley, Lesly.

Listen to the Name

If the way your child's name sounds is important to you, listen to its music. Names like Pat Mack, which combine two single syllables, can sound curt and less pleasing than, for example, Jennifer Mack. The most melodious names are often those with unequal numbers of syllables. Thus, John David Madigan and Virginia Beth Northrop are tapping the right tune. Alliteration, the repetition of the first sound, can be fun: Susan Swenson and Tom Tarinelli will always have agreeable names (and bookends with matching initials). But sometimes, sound can take over sense: Being called Jason Mason is not the easiest way to go through life.

Lester Phonetic form of English place name "Leicester." Les.

Levi (*Hebrew*): Joined; attached. Levin, Levon.

Lewis English form of Louis (*Old German/French*): Renowned warrior. Lew.

Lionel (*Latin*): Young lion. Lionello.

Lloyd (*Welsh*): Grey, or holy. Floyd.

Lorne Variation of Lawrence (*Latin*): From Laurentium. Lorn.

Louis (*Old German/French*): Renowned warrior. Ludwig, Luigi, Luis.

Lowell (*Old French*): Young wolf. Lowe, Lowel, Lovell.

Luke (*Greek*): From Lucania. Lucas, Lucien, Lucky.

Lyle (*Old French*): Island dweller. Lisle, Lyell.

Lyndon (*Old English*): Hill with lime trees. Lynden, Lindon, Lin.

Mac (*Scottish*): Son of Mack. Mackey.

Madison (*Old English*): Son of mighty warrior. Maddy, Madisson.

Malcolm (*Irish/Scottish*): Servant of St. Columbus. Malcolum.

Manning (*Old English*): Son of the man. Manny.

Manuel Diminutive of Emanuel (*Hebrew*): God is with us. Mano, Manolo.

Marc French form of Mark (*Latin*): Warlike.

Marcus (*Latin*): Warlike. Marco, Markus.

Mario Italian version of Mark.

Mark (*Latin*): Warlike.

Marshall (*Old French*): Horse tender. Also Scottish occupational name. Marsh, Marshell.

Martin (*Latin*): From Mars, the god of war. Marten, Marty.

Marvin (*Uncertain origin*): Marve, Mervin.

Matthew (*Hebrew*): Gift of the Lord. Matt, Mathew, Mathias.

Maurice (*Latin*): Moorish; dark-skinned. Maurie, Morris, Morice.

Max Diminutive of Maxmillian (*Latin*): Greatest.

Maxwell (*Scottish*): Place name. Maccus's well. Max.

Melvin (*Uncertain origin*): Mel, Melvyn.

Michael (*Hebrew*): Who is like the Lord? Mike, Mikey, Michal.

Miles (*Old German*): Generous. Form of Emil (*Latin*): Eager to please.

Milton (*Old English*): Mill town. Milt, Mylton.

Mitchell (*Middle English*): Variation of Michael. Mitch, Mitchel.

Mohammed (*Arabic*): Highly praised. Muhammad, Muhammed.

Mordecai (*Hebrew*): Uncertain meaning. Mort.

Morris Anglicization of Maurice. Morrison.

Mortimer (*Old French*): Still water. Mort, Morty.

Morgan (*Welsh*): Great; bright.

Moses (*Hebrew*): Savior, or taken from the water. Moshe.

Murray (*Scottish*): Place name. Moray.

Myron (*Greek*): Fragrant oil.

Nadim (*Arabic*): Friend.

Nathan (*Hebrew*): Given. Nat, Nate.

Nathaniel (*Hebrew*): God has given. Nate, Nathanial.

Ned Pet name for Edward (*Old English*): Wealthy defender, and Edmond (*Old English*): Wealthy protector.

Neil (*Irish*): Champion. Neal, Neall.

Nelson (*English*): Son of Neil. Nealson, Nilson.

Nicholas (*Greek*): People of victory. Colin, Nick, Nicolis.

Noah: (*Uncertain origin*): Rest, or long-lived, or wandering.

Noel (*French*): Christmas.

Nolan (*Irish*): Famous. Noland, Nolen.

Norman (*Old English*): From the North. Norm, Normand.

Norton (*English*): Northern town. Nort.

Nuri (*Arabic*): Light. Noori, Nuris, Nur.

Oliver (*Latin*): Olive. Ollie, Olivor.

Omar (*Arabic*): Expressive; eloquent.

Oren (*Irish*): Green. Orrin, Oren.

Orson (*Latin*): Bearlike. Orsen, Orsini, Sonny.

Osborn (*Old English*): Divine bear.

Oscar (*Old English*): God-spear. Oskar, Ozzy.

Otis (*Old English*): Son of Otto. Oates.

Owen (*Greek*): Well-born. Welsh form of Eugene. Ewen, Owin.

Patrick (*Latin*): Noble man. Pat, Patric, Paddy, Patton.

Paul (*Latin*): Small. Paolo, Paulie, Pavel.

Peter (*Greek*): Rock. Pedro, Pietro.

Peyton (*Old English*): Place name. Fighting man's estate. Payton.

Philip (*Greek*): Lover of horses. Phillip, Felipe, Phil.

Pierce Variation of Peter (*Greek*): Rock. Pearce, Piers, Pierson.

Porter (*Latin*): Gatekeeper.

Prescott (*Old English*): Place name. Priest's cottage. Prescot, Prestcott.

Preston (*Old English*): Place name. Priest's settlement.

Quentin (*Latin*): Fifth. Quintin.

Quincy (*Old French*): Estate of the fifth son. Quincey.

Quinn (*Irish*): Uncertain meaning.

Ralph (*Old English*): Wolf-counsel. Rolf, Raoul, Rafe.

Rafi (*Arabic*): Holding high. Rafee, Raffi.

Randall (*Old English*): Wolf-shield. Randel, Randal, Randy.

Randolph (*Old English*): Wolf-shield. Randy.

Raphael (*Hebrew*): God has healed. Rafael, Rafe, Rafello.

Rashid (*Turkish*): Righteous. Rasheed, Rasheid.

Ravi (*Hindi*): Sun. Ravee.

Raymond (*Old German*): Counselor; protector. Ramon, Ramounde, Ray.

Reed (*Old English*): Red-haired. Reid, Read, Reade.

Reginald (*Old English*): Powerful force. Reggie, Reinhold, Reynold.

Reuben (*Hebrew*): Behold! A son! Rubin, Rueben, Ruben, Reuven.

Reynolds (*Old English*): Counsel; power. Form of Reginald. Reynold, Rinaldo, Renault.

Richard (*Old German*): Strong ruler. Pet forms include Dick, Rich, Ricky, Rico.

Riley (*Irish*): Valiant. Reilly.

Robert (*Old German*): Bright fame. Bob, Robin, Roberto, Bert, Robby.

Roderick (*Old German*): Famous rule. Broderick, Rodd, Rory.

Rodney (*Old English*): Place name. Island near the clearing. Rodnie.

Roger (*Old German*): Famous spearman. Rodger, Rogers, Ruggiero.

Roland (*Old German*): Famous land. Lanny, Rollin, Rowland.

Ronald (*Old English*): Powerful force. Form of Reginald. Ranald, Ron, Ronny.

Rory (*Gaelic*): Red.

Ross (*Scottish*): Place name. Headland. Rosse, Rossell.

Roy (*Gaelic*): Red, or (*French*): King. Roydon, Elroy, Rey, Roi.

Rudolph (*Old German*): Famous wolf. Rudolf, Rudi, Rudy, Rolf.

Rupert German form of Robert (*Old German*): Ruprecht.

Russell (*Old French*): Red haired. Russ, Russel, Roussell.

Ryan (*Irish*): Uncertain meaning. Ryon, Ryun.

Ryder (*Old English*): Horseman. Rider, Ridder.

Salim (*Arabic*): Happy. Saleem, Salem.

Salvatore (*Italian*): Sal, Salvador, Xavier, Zavior.

Samuel (*Hebrew*): Heard by God. Sam, Sammy, Shem.

Sanford (*Old English*): Place name. Sandy ford. Sandford.

Saul (*Hebrew*): Asked for. Sol, Sollie.

Schuyler (*Dutch*): Shield, or scholar. Skyler, Schuylar.

Scott (*Old English*): A Scotsman. Scottie, Scot, Scotty.

Sean Irish form of John (*Hebrew*): God is gracious. Shawn, Shane, Shaun.

Sebastian (*Latin*): From Sebastia. Seb, Bastien, Sebastien, Bastian.

Seth (*Hebrew*): To put; set.

Shane (*Irish*): Shayne, Shaine.

Sharif (*Arabic*): Honest. Shareef.

Sheldon (*Old English*): Place name. Steep valley. Shelden, Sheldin.

Sherman (*Old English*): Occupational name. One who shears. Shermann, Scherman.

Seymour (*Old French*): From St. Maur. Seamore, Morey, Morrie.

Sidney (*Old French*): From St. Denis. Sid, Sydney.

Simon (*Hebrew*): Listening well. Si, Simeon, Simmons, Simpson.

Sloan (*Irish*): Man of arms. Sloane.

Spencer (*Middle English*): Provisioner. Spence, Spenser.

Stanley (*Old English*): Stony field. Stan, Stanleigh, Stanly.

Stephen (*Greek*): Crown. Stephan, Steven, Estefan, Stevie.

How excellent is thy name in all the earth.

THE BOOK OF PSALMS

Sterling (*Old English*): Genuine; of excellent quality. Stirling.

Stuart (*Old English*): Occupational name; steward. Stewart, Steward.

Sylvester (*Latin*): Wooded; rural. Silvester.

Tahir (*Arabic*): Pure. Taheer.

Terence (*Latin*): Polished. Terrance, Terrence, Terry.

Theodore (*Greek*): Gift of God. Ted, Teddy, Theo, Theodor.

Thomas (*Aramaic*): Twin. Tomas, Thomson, Thompson, Tom, Tommy.

Timothy (*Greek*): Honoring God. Tim, Timon, Timmy, Timmothy.

Tobias (*Hebrew*): God is good. Tobe, Tobey, Tobin, Toby.

Townsend (*Old English*): Place name. End of town.

Travis (*Old French*): Toll collector. Traver, Travers, Travys.

Trent (*Latin*): Gushing waters. River place name. Trenton, Trentin.

Trevor (*Welsh*): Great homestead. Trefor, Trevar, Trever.

Troy (*Irish*): Foot soldier. Troye, Troi.

Tucker (*Old English*): Occupational name. Fabric pleater.

Tyler (*Old English*): Occupational name. Tile maker. Tylar, Tilar, Ty.

Tyrone (*Irish*): Land of Owen. Ty, Tye.

Ulysses (*Greek*): Wrathful. Ulises, Ulisse.

Upton (*Old English*): Place name. Upper forest.

Uriel (*Hebrew*): Flame of God.

Valentine (*Latin*): Strong. Val, Valentin, Valentino.

Van (*Dutch*): Of, or from. Possibly a pet form of Vance or Vanya. Vann.

Vance (*Old English*): Place name. Marshland.

Vaughn (*Welsh*): Little. Vaughan.

Vernon (*Old French*): Place name. Alder grove. Vern, Verne, Lavern.

Victor (*Latin*): Conqueror. Vic, Vick, Vittorio.

Vincent (*Latin*): Conquering. Vincente, Vincenzo, Vinny, Vin, Vince.

Wade (*Old English*): Place name. River ford. Wayde.

Walker (*Old English*): Occupational name. One who walks on wool.

Wallace (*Old English*): Welshman. Wallis.

Walter (*Old German*): Ruling people. Walt.

Ward (*Old English*): Occupational name. Watchman. Warde, Warden.

Warren (*Old German*): Defender. Ware, Waring, Warrin.

Wayne (*Old English*): Occupational name. Wagon builder or driver. Wayn.

Wesley (*Old English*): Place name. Western meadow. Wes, Westleigh, Westly.

Wilbur (*Old German*): Uncertain meaning. Wilber, Willbur.

William (*Old German*): Will; helmet. Bill, Billy, Will, Willy, Wilmer.

Wilson (*Old English*): Son of Will. Willson, Will.

Winston (*Old English*): Place name. Friend's town. Wynston.

Winthrop (*Old English*): Place name. Friend's village.

Woodrow (*Old English*): Row by the woods. Woody.

Wyatt (*Old French*): Small fighter. Wiatt, Wye.

Xavier (*Basque*): New house. Zavier.

Yves (*French*): Form of Ivo (*Old German*): Archer. Ives, Yvo.

Zachary (*Hebrew*): The Lord has remembered. Zachariah, Zack, Zach.

Zane English form of John (*Hebrew*): The Lord is gracious. Zayne.